Yucky Animals in the Yard

Alix Wood

WINDMILL BOOKS

New York

Published in 2014 by Windmill Books, An Imprint of Rosen Publishing
29 East 21st Street, New York, NY 10010

Editor: Sara Howell
Designer: Alix Wood
Consultant: Sally Morgan

Photo Credits: Cover, 1, 3, 4, 5, 6, 7, 8 top, 10, 11, 12 top, 13, 14, 15 top, 16, 18, 19 bottom, 20, 21 middle and bottom, 23 bottom, 24, 25, 26, 27, 28, 29 top © Shutterstock; 8 bottom © Julio Ospinao, 9 top © Takahashi; 9 bottom © Darios44/Fotolia; 12 bottom © lightpoet/Fotolia; 15 bottom © and 17 top © Eric Isselée; 17 bottom © Hectonichus; 19 top © goodluz/Fotolia; 21 top © Aaron Ashall/Fotolia; 22 Vive Images/Fotolia; 23 top © alessandrozocc/Fotolia; 29 bottom © Room 237.

Library of Congress Cataloging-in-Publication Data

Wood, Alix.
 Yucky animals in the yard / by Alix Wood.
     pages cm. — (Earth's grossest animals)
 Includes index.
 ISBN 978-1-61533-731-6 (library binding) — ISBN 978-1-61533-779-8 (pbk.) —
 ISBN 978-1-61533-780-4 (6-pack)
 1. Garden animals—Juvenile literature. 2. Urban animals—Juvenile literature. I. Title.
 QL119.W656 2014
 591.75′6—dc23
                              2012046826

Manufactured in the United States of America

CPSIA Compliance Information: Batch #BS13WM: For Further Information contact: Windmill Books, New York, New York at 1-866-478-0556

Contents

Yuck in Your Yard

What horrors lurk in your yard? That kind of depends on where you live. Wherever that is, though, you're sure to find some pretty nasty creatures!

Go outside and take a good look. Lots of creatures have set up home in your backyard. You know your family dog is in your yard, but do you know how gross a dog can be? Some creatures are pretty small. You'll need to look a little harder to find them. But maybe you won't want to, once you've found out a little more about their revolting habits!

What's worse than biting into a pear and finding a **larvae**? Biting into a pear and finding half a larvae! That's gross.

Your pet rabbit seems cute until it starts eating its own waste! Male rabbits often spray their **urine** over the female and young to mark them as belonging to "his" social group.

Fossils of cockroaches have been found that are 300 million years old!

Cockroaches live in the yard in warm weather, but can survive freezing temperatures. In cold weather they like to come inside. They can live for a long time without food or water, making them very hard to destroy. They carry disease and can cause **allergies** in humans.

Gross Bugs and Beetles

There are plenty of revolting bugs and beetles in your yard. The stinky shield bug will give off a vile smell when attacked. Then again, the bug that kills the shield bug is even worse!

Shield bugs, often called stink bugs, have **glands** between their first and second pair of legs that produce a foul-smelling liquid, smelling something like ten-day-old socks. This smell stops **predators** from wanting to eat them. Stink bugs release their odor when chased, picked up, or stepped on, so they are kind of hard to get rid of!

Stink bugs live in countries such as the United States, Japan, Taiwan, and China. In cold weather they like to come inside buildings!

The assassin bug stalks other insects. It uses its needlelike beak to stab its prey and inject poisons that can **paralyze** prey and turns its body to mush! This liquid-like mush is then sucked out with the assassin bug's straw-like mouthparts. One species bites people. They are called "kissing bugs" because they like tender flesh, such as the lips of sleeping humans.

an assassin beetle killing a shield bug

A burying beetle (right) buries dead birds and rodents as food for its larvae. It covers the carcass with fluid from its body to slow down the decay. Then it lines the hole with fur or feathers and lays its eggs. The beetle helps feed the larvae by eating and vomiting back up the rotting flesh!

Club-like antennae can sniff out dead animals far away.

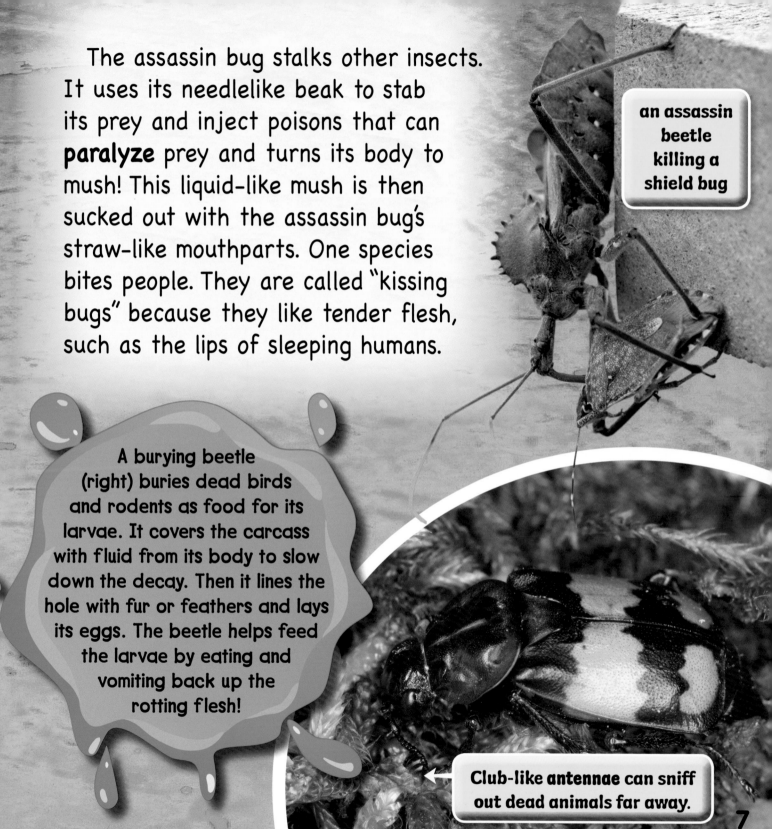

Things That Sting!

Insects bite and sting when they are annoyed and need to defend themselves, or they bite and sting to feed. It's dangerous out in the yard!

One type of wasp will even pick a fight with a deadly tarantula. The female tarantula hawk (below) stings and paralyzes the spider and drags it to her burrow. She lays an egg on the spider's abdomen. The larva hatches and feeds on the spider. It avoids vital organs so the spider stays alive. When the wasp becomes an adult, it leaves the spider.

The Asian giant hornet is the world's largest hornet. It's around 2 inches (50 mm) long! It has a **venomous** sting which can dissolve flesh. In Japan it is called the giant sparrow bee.

A tarantula hawk catches a tarantula.

Asian giant hornets can easily defeat a honeybee colony, but Japanese honeybees have a plan! They gather near the entrance of the nest and set a trap. As the hornet enters, hundreds of honeybees surround it, in a ball. The bees violently vibrate, which raises the temperature and the level of **carbon dioxide** in the ball. The hornet cannot survive this combination and dies!

These Japanese honeybees form a "bee ball" around two hornets.

A beekeeper knows how to handle his bees gently.

When a honeybee stings, it kills the bee. Its stinger is pulled from its body, along with some of the bee's insides.

Your Family Pet

Many of our family pets will spend some or all their time out in our yards. Some of them have pretty gross habits!

A dog can do some pretty revolting things, like roll in dead animals or animal waste. Why? One theory is this "perfume" makes the dog more interesting to other dogs. They certainly like to sniff each other's behinds when introduced! Another reason may be it disguises their own smell, so they can hunt better.

Some dogs eat animal waste, too! Vets are not sure why. It may be a habit picked up when they were puppies, or maybe they like the **undigested** food in the waste.

A male cat sprays urine to communicate with other cats. Cats also leave scent signals by rubbing and scratching against things. The scent lets other cats know that another cat has been there and marks the area with the cat's own familiar smell. Female cats spray urine to attract males when they want to **mate**, too.

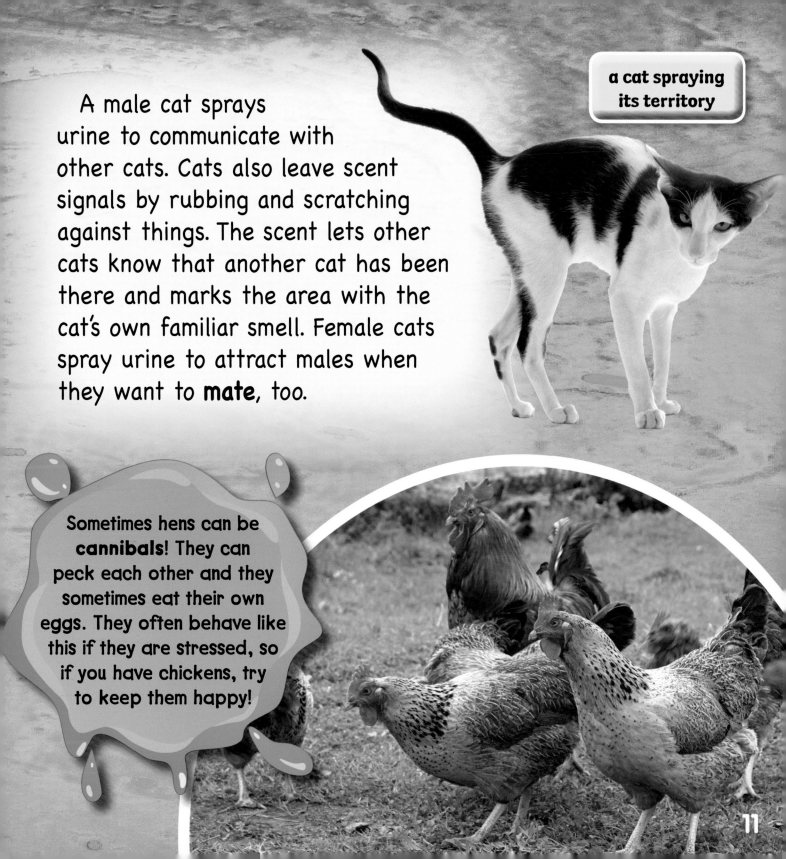

a cat spraying its territory

Sometimes hens can be **cannibals**! They can peck each other and they sometimes eat their own eggs. They often behave like this if they are stressed, so if you have chickens, try to keep them happy!

Animals With Spikes

Porcupines and hedgehogs look cute, but they are not so cuddly if you get a face full of their needlelike quills or spines!

Porcupines live in Africa, Asia, North America, and South America. The African porcupine has quills nearly 1 foot (30 cm) long! Quills are sharp and have tiny barbs on their tips which make them hard to remove. If threatened, a porcupine attacks by moving backward or sideways into its enemy. The quills easily pull loose from the porcupine and get stuck in the attacker's skin. Within a few weeks, the porcupine will grow back the lost quills.

The average porcupine has around 30,000 quills on its body.

12

Hedgehogs live in Europe. If attacked, they roll into a ball and tighten two large muscles that run down either side of their body. This makes their spines raise up. The muscles pull different spines in different directions, so they crisscross each other, making a very effective defense.

These young hedgehogs are rolled into a defensive pose.

Hedgehogs are skilled climbers, but are not great at getting themselves back down again! Instead, they roll into a ball and drop, using their spines to cushion the fall!

Smelly Creatures

In general, things won't want to eat you if you smell really bad. Several animals in the yard use that to their advantage and they smell horrible!

Millipedes may look harmless, but many types of millipede carry secret **chemical** weapons! They have stink glands which emit a foul-smelling, foul-tasting compound. Some species release cyanide, a deadly poison!

The chemicals produced by some millipedes can burn or blister the skin. Always wash your hands after holding a millipede, just to be safe.

When threatened, a millipede will coil its body into a spiral to protect its soft underside.

This cute little bombardier beetle sprays boiling, stinky liquid and **toxic** fluid at you if you annoy it! This liquid can kill an insect and is painful to human skin. The African species of bombardier beetle can swivel its firing chamber through 270° so it is pinpoint accurate!

If threatened, a skunk can spray a really smelly oily liquid from glands under its large tail. It can spray as far as 10 feet (3 m). The spray smells terrible and is almost impossible to remove. Most types of skunk live in North America and South America, except the Asian stink badger.

This skunk is getting ready to fire!

Home Wreckers

There are a few tiny creatures in your yard that can make a big mess of your home. Carpenter ants, longhorn beetle larvae, and termites all love to eat away at wood.

Carpenter ants like moist, decaying, or hollow wood. They cut passageways in the wood so they can move around within it. Wooden parts of a house, like windows, roof eaves, decks, and porches can become infested by carpenter ants.

damage done by carpenter ants

Some carpenter ants have a funny way of defending themselves. They explode! If an ant senses it is losing a fight, it produces a glue from a large gland in its body. The glue bursts out and entangles the attacker. Exploding obviously also kills the carpenter ant.

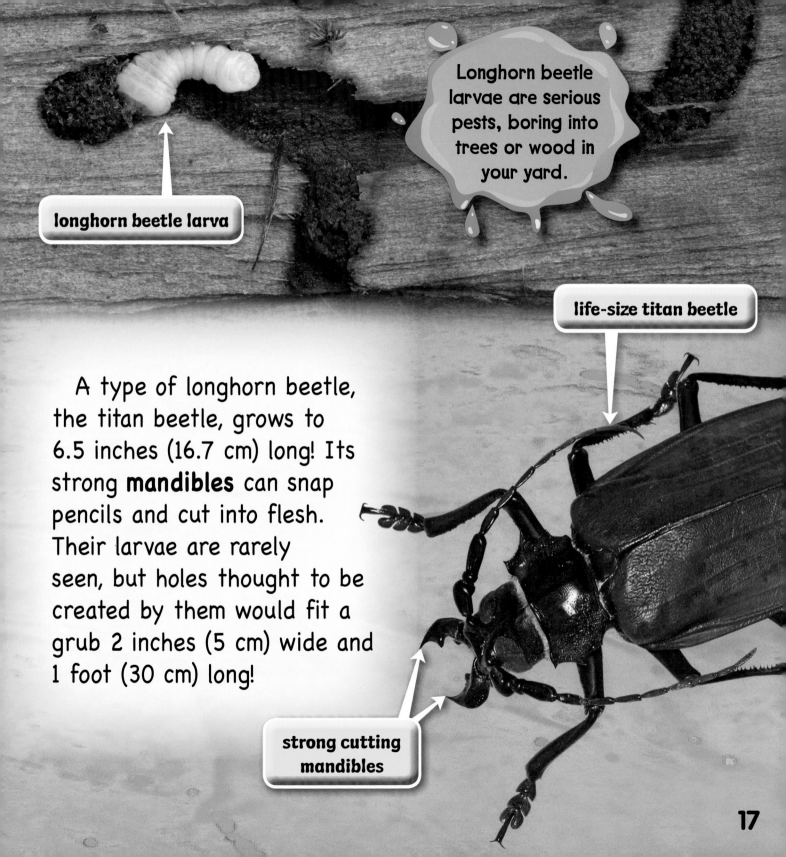

longhorn beetle larva

Longhorn beetle larvae are serious pests, boring into trees or wood in your yard.

life-size titan beetle

A type of longhorn beetle, the titan beetle, grows to 6.5 inches (16.7 cm) long! Its strong **mandibles** can snap pencils and cut into flesh. Their larvae are rarely seen, but holes thought to be created by them would fit a grub 2 inches (5 cm) wide and 1 foot (30 cm) long!

strong cutting mandibles

Poisonous Pests

Animals such as scorpions, and even some toads, can be poisonous. You wouldn't think a grasshopper could harm you, but in some country's backyards, grasshoppers make toxic foam!

Scorpions have a poisonous sting in their tail. The Arizona bark scorpion is small, but its venom causes severe pain, loss of breathing, the feeling of being electrocuted, inability to move, fits, and eventually can cause death.

This desert hairy scorpion's hairs help it detect prey vibrating the soil.

stinger

If you get stung, clean the sting site with soap and water, apply a cool compress, and get medical help. Raising the sting site above heart level is a good idea, too.

pincers

Many toads are poisonous. When the toads are threatened, their glands secrete a milky-white poisonous fluid. Pets can often be harmed by their poison.

a cane toad

If you live in Central America, South America, or Australia you may have a cane toad in your yard. People have died from eating cane toads. Their skin is toxic. The tadpoles are highly toxic, too.

The foam grasshopper lives in South Africa and can produce a toxic foam from glands in its body. The foam smells foul and surrounds the grasshopper in a protective umbrella about 3.3 feet (1 m) around it.

This foam grasshopper is feeding on berries, but they also eat milkweed, which is what makes their foam toxic.

Tongue and Tail Tricks

Lizards can do some gross things. Chameleons have sticky, suction cup tongues, lizards can break off pieces of their body, and blue-tongued skinks just look strange.

Chameleons live in backyards in areas of Europe, Africa, and Asia. This small reptile has a very long tongue. In fact, its tongue is nearly three-quarters the length of its body! It uses its sticky tongue to catch prey. It can even grip lizards nearly the same size as itself. The muscles under the tip of a chameleon's tongue act like a suction cup, and the tongue is covered in kind of sticky glue.

A baby veiled chameleon is catching a fly with its tongue.

Many lizards can drop their tail if they are being attacked. The tail breaks off at specially designed "fracture plane" which doesn't harm the lizard. Then the tail wiggles around on the ground. Ugh!

The wriggling tail distracts the predator, and the lizard can escape. Its tail will eventually grow back.

a lizard's tail growing back

The blue-tongued skink (right) lives in Australia. It is generally shy, but if threatened, it puffs up its body, sticks out its long, blue tongue, and hisses! A skink can drop its tail, too.

Really Slimy Creatures

There's something really horrible about slime. And there's a lot of it in the yard. Here are some seriously slimy creatures.

This slimy-looking salamander (below) needs to keep its skin moist or it may die. Like lizards, salamanders have a disposable tail. If threatened, they raise their body, lower their head, and wave their tail around. They release a smelly, sticky liquid, and they can bite.

A relative of the salamander, the ribbed newt, has needlelike rib tips. If attacked, it squeezes its muscles and the rib tips pierce through its skin to stab its enemy!

a speckled black salamander

Slime helps slugs find a partner (right) as it contains a chemical which attracts mates. They can follow the slime trail to meet the chemical's producer!

A slug's slime soaks up water, which is why it's nearly impossible to wash it off your hands.

Snail and slug slime coats the ground like a silvery track, which makes it easier for the animal to glide along. The stickiness helps them climb up things, too, and it keeps the slug or snail moist. Slime also repulses predators.

Slithering Snakes

Many people are scared of snakes. There are venomous snakes in most countries of the world. Snakes shed their skin several times a year, eat their prey whole, and their venom could kill you!

venom

rattle

shed snake skin

A rattlesnake (left) rattles to warn other animals to leave it alone. It grows a new piece of rattle when it sheds its skin. It makes a rattling noise when two segments knock together. Baby rattlesnakes can't rattle as they only have one segment!

To shed its skin, a snake rubs its head against a rock to split the skin. The skin peels back until the snake is able to wiggle out of it.

Snakes have flexible jaws, which allows them to swallow animals much larger than themselves. Their backward-curving teeth grip the animal as they swallow it. Some snakes aren't venomous, but that doesn't mean they can't kill prey. The boa constrictor (below) squeezes its prey until it suffocates.

a garter snake eating a large fish

Snakes inject venom into their prey with their hollow teeth, called fangs. When a snake strikes, venom is squeezed from a gland under each eye into the fang.

Boa constrictors can grow to nearly 13 feet (4 m) long!

Creepy Spiders

A lot of people think all spiders are gross! But there's no arguing that these specimens are certainly ones to steer clear of!

Tarantulas are not just big, they're deadly. The biggest tarantulas can kill animals as large as lizards, mice, birds, and small snakes. They can be found in backyards in the southern and western United States, Central America, and South America.

Tarantulas produce silk from their feet — all eight of them! They're so big and heavy, the silk from their feet helps them grip as they climb up walls.

a life-size Mexican redknee tarantula

Another terror lurking in many North American backyards is the recluse spider or "fiddle-back." It has a really nasty bite which leaves a decaying wound that takes a long time to heal. The recluse often hides in bedding or clothing.

recluse spider

The black widow spider is very small, but very deadly. It doesn't look for trouble, but if you accidentally touch its hourglass-shaped web, it will bite. Black widow venom causes painful cramps, interferes with breathing, and shuts down areas of the body.

Widow spiders can be pretty dangerous to each other, too. The Australian redback is the black widow's cousin. The female spider eats the male during mating! And the redback male helps this happen by moving his body toward her mouth!

a life-size Australian redback

27

Playing Dead

If you find a lifeless animal in your yard, it may not be dead. Some animals "play dead" to confuse predators. Predators usually only like live prey, as dead prey may have a disease they could catch.

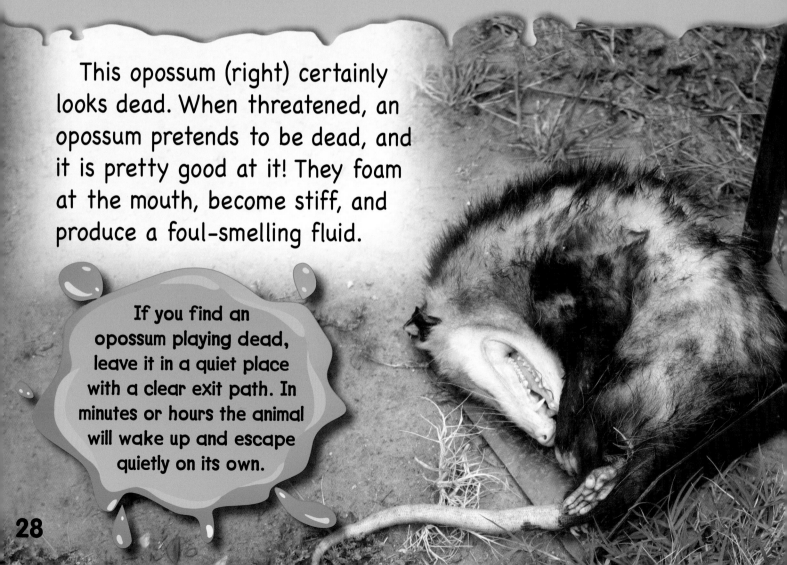

This opossum (right) certainly looks dead. When threatened, an opossum pretends to be dead, and it is pretty good at it! They foam at the mouth, become stiff, and produce a foul-smelling fluid.

If you find an opossum playing dead, leave it in a quiet place with a clear exit path. In minutes or hours the animal will wake up and escape quietly on its own.

a toad playing dead

Toads play dead if they meet a predator, too. They also sometimes puff up their bodies to look bigger than they actually are.

The horned lizard has a really gross way of staying safe from predators. They squirt a stream of blood from around their eyes! Their first defense is to stand still, but if that doesn't work, they run in short bursts and stop suddenly to confuse the predator. If this fails, they puff themselves up to look larger and more difficult to swallow.

Horned lizards can squirt their stream of blood up to 5 feet (1.5 m). The blood tastes foul to dogs and cats.

a horned lizard squirting blood

Glossary

allergies (A-lur-jeez)
Abnormal reactions to substances, often causing sneezing, itching, or rashes.

antennae (an-TEH-nee)
A pair of movable feelers on an insect's head.

cannibals (KA-nih-bulz)
Human beings or animals that eat their own kind.

carbon dioxide (KAHR-bun dy-OK-syd)
An odorless, colorless gas. People breathe out carbon dioxide.

chemical (KEH-mih-kul)
An element, compound, or mixture of elements and compounds. Chemicals may be solids, liquids, or gases.

glands (GLANDZ)
Organs that make and secrete saliva, sweat, or bile from a plant or animal body.

larvae (LAHR-vee)
Young wingless forms that hatch from eggs of many insects.

mandibles (MAN-dih-bulz)
The mouthparts of some insects or crustacea that often form biting organs.

mate (MAYT)
To come together
in order to have young.

paralyze (PER-uh-lyz)
To make powerless or
unable to act, function,
or move.

predators (PREH-duh-terz)
Animals that live by killing
and eating other animals.

toxic (TOK-sik)
Of a poisonous substance
produced by a living
organism that is poisonous
to other organisms.

undigested
(un-dy-JES-ted)
Food that has not been
used by the body.

urine (YUR-un)
Animal waste that is
usually a yellowish liquid in
mammals but semisolid in
birds and reptiles.

venomous (VEH-nuh-mis)
Having or producing poison.

WEBSITES
For web resources related to the
subject of this book, go to:
www.windmillbooks.com/weblinks
and select this book's title.

Read More

Antill, Sara. *Porcupines*. Unusual Animals. New York: Windmill Books, 2011.

Clark, Willow. *Rattlesnake!*. Animal Danger Zone. New York: Windmill Books, 2011.

Simon, Seymour. *Spiders*. New York: HarperCollins, 2008.

Index

12-'14